For Evangeline

Clouds and More Clouds

*Peace &
Light,*

David H. Rosen

DHR

Foreword by Vincent Tripi
Illustration by Alec Formatin Shirley

LILY POOL PRESS

© 2013 David H. Rosen
drdavidhrosen@gmail.com

ISBN: 978-1-62890-807-7

For Lanara,
Love of my life

An autumn night=
don't think your life
didn't matter

=Basho

Foreword

Dear David,

    We've had a classic New England blizzard & everything is reduced & expanded at the same time. Self & other. It causes me to think of the poem that is written in simplicity, which must be written again & again because it brings us to the centre, makes us familiar with the Nature of things . . . makes us alive with ourselves. Was this what you had in mind when you wrote:

> First spring day
> the fawn startled by
> everything

    Ah the consciousness of freedom! The possibilities of poetry!

There is an intimacy of exchange between fawn & world that becomes our intimacy. Alertness is conferred upon the reader & in a mysterious way all our uncollected alertnesses can fit into one. The well framed image of the startled fawn brings me to the very limit of what i am able to understand & inevitably have no need to understand. We are tiny in the changing world while at the same time great in the eyes of the fawn who humbles us with its innocence & vulnerability. i am vulnerable to the poem.

Which reminds me. i very much enjoy the way in which, through words & magic, you are able again & again to move from universal to particular, particular to universal . . . to the Way.

There is a lesson in this book. Archetypal & rejuvenating= connectedness with everything & at the same time the impermanence of it all. i use the following as examples:

> Orange blossoms
> a hummingbird
> orange blossom

or

> two men in wheelchairs
> feeding the sparrows
> one sparrow

i know that you began to write haiku because that was one realm in particular by which you sought to understand. You would not allow it to elude you completely. You had no choice.

Someone once said of Giacometti, "He will either go very far or go mad." You have gone very far. Almost wild. And as you say:

> Wild . . .
> no further proof
> of God

So i say thank you David for this Collection. Thank you for a well-needed resting place. A place proportionate to our need for Origins. A place where we are assured of enough wood to carry us through those classic New England blizzards, whenever & however they may come.

vincent tripi
February 2013
Greenfield, Mass.

Clouds and More Clouds

First spring day
the fawn startled by
everything

Wild . . .
no further proof
of God

In an oak grove
a Buddha
no saplings

Orange blossoms
a hummingbird
orange blossom

All leaves
fall
day my father died

Almost full moon
the scent of one magnolia
two

Two Douglas firs
always been touching
my marriage

= *for Lanara*

Seed to bloom
your zinnia?
my zinnia?

Finally
looking at a peony
speechless

A moonlit way . . .
no stumps
the silence of trees

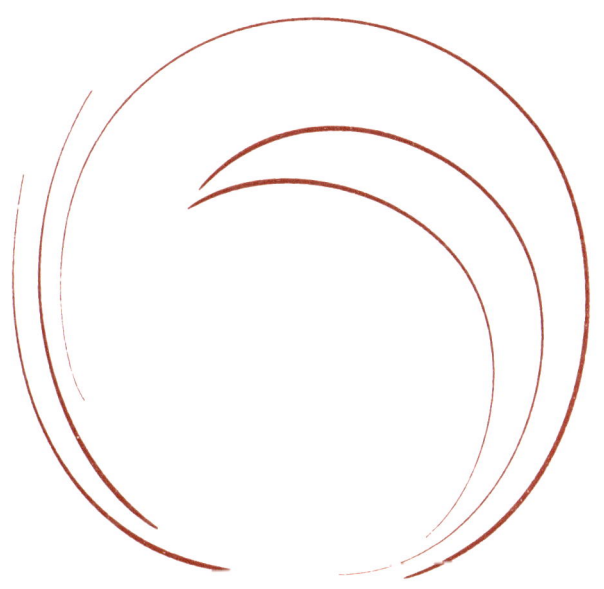

Mother dying . . .
full moon over
Kansas City, the world

Red cardinal atop
leafless gingko
year of emptiness

Thank you
for keeping me warm
without being here

Clouds
and more clouds
lone black bird

Indian summer =
upside-down mantis
on path

Two men in wheelchairs
feeding the sparrows
one sparrow

Leaving academia . . .
I join my friends
birds, trees, and wind

Dr. Nada
my card
blank

Last autumn day
pomegranates
and their seeds

Fall equinox=
ripe persimmons
mosquito joins us

Bent tree
among bent trees
sauntering through the woods

Limbs of the live oak
touch the grass
lazy September Sunday

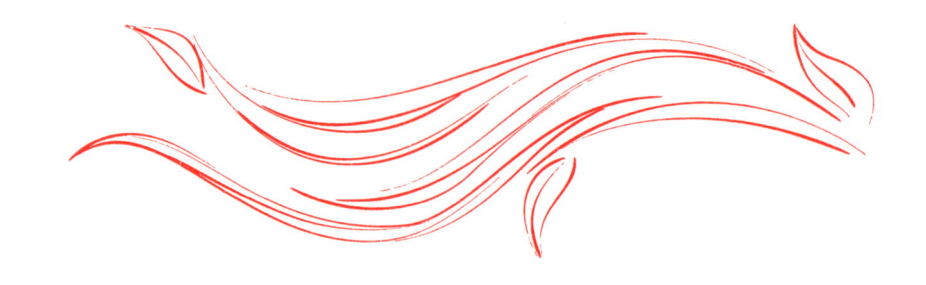

Gray fox
startled by
a single rustling leaf

Dead tree
brought to life
red-headed woodpeckers

Alone
until you returned
red dragonfly

My life
a long, slow rain
earth

The spider web
mysterious spiral
life and death

Trekking up the hill . . .
suddenly looking up
a new year

ON MOTHER EARTH

Oh, Earth is patient,
and Earth is old . . .
> = *Sophocles*

On mother earth =
Every breath
Simple and easy

On mother earth =
Universal tree
Upside down roots

On mother earth =
Each spring
Pure and flowing

On mother earth =
Giant oaks and
Their shadows

On mother earth =
Ever present sun's rays and
Moonbeams

On mother earth =
A puppy
Wants to play

On mother earth =
Verdant ferns
Along the path

On mother earth =
After rain
Sunbeam appears

On mother earth =
Deep cave
Black with light

On mother earth =
Every step
Gentle and measured

Madly Sobering

> *It is more important to know what sort of person has a disease than to know what sort of disease a person has.* = Hippocrates

I'd fallen, so I was referred to a specialist. Having had a similar dream image that same morning, I asked my neurologist, Dr. Joan Jensen, "What are all those white spots in the MRI of my brain?" In her direct, yet kind way, she said, "Those are scars." "Scars?" She responded, "Yes, sclerosis means scar." I nearly fell off the chair. Then she added, "MS is not a death sentence." That was two years ago and I started taking medication and drastically changed my diet and life style. I recall the accurate and shocking response of my New Zealand poet friend, Ralph Woodward, "Madly Sobering." Comforting were the wise words of James Hillman, "A scar is the mark of soul in flesh." Hence, it's contact with the ancestors: Multiple Souls.

> Light
> in the darkness
> the black sun

Worth trying
at least once
being nobody in Bassersdorf

Teeter tater . . .
I know
what do you know?

CREDITS

The Basho haiku comes from Robert Hass, "The Essential Haiku: Versions of Basho, Buson & Issa. Hopewell, NJ: THE ECCO PRESS, 1994, p. 7.

"Alone" = HSA Anthology 2005 "Loose Change."
"Finally" = Frogpond 2009
"Red cardinal" = Modern Haiku 2009
"Thank you..." = HSA Anthol. 2006 "Fish in Love."
"Clouds" = Modern Haiku 2012
"Leaving academia" = Frogpond 2009
"Limbs..." Modern Haiku 2008
"My life" = Frogpond 2011

The Haibun "Madly Sobering" = Frogpond 2012 (with the quote by Hippocrates) "black sun" refers to alchemic and Hermetic traditions. Suns can correspond to gold, generative masculine principles, or the divine spark in man.

"On Mother earth . . ." series = Psychological Perspectives 2012, 55:372-373 (The quote by Sophocles is from Antigone).

About the Author

David H. Rosen, M.D., is a psychiatrist and Jungian analyst who was the first holder of the McMillan Professorship in Analytical Psychology at Texas A&M University. He is the author of many publications, including eight books and numerous articles, chapters, essays, and haiku poems. He now lives in Eugene, Oregon, and is an Affiliate Professor in Psychiatry at Oregon Health & Science University.

Colophon

Three hundred copies were printed at Swamp Press using Pastonchi, cast in house, on a Heidelberg Windmill. The text is Pastelle, the cover is Stardream Sapphire. Smyth sewing was done on an antique No. 3.